THE VIRGIN & THE NIGHTINGALE

Fleur Adcock was born in New Zealand in 1934. She spent the war years in England, returning with her family to New Zealand in 1947. She emigrated to Britain in 1963, working as a librarian in London until 1979. In 1977-78 she was writer-in-residence at Charlotte Mason College of Education, Ambleside. She was Northern Arts Literary Fellow in 1979-81, living in Newcastle, becoming a freelance writer after her return to London. She received an OBE in 1996, and the Queen's Gold Medal for Poetry in 2006 for *Poems 1960-2000* (Bloodaxe Books, 2000).

Fleur Adcock published three pamphlets with Bloodaxe: *Below Loughrigg* (1979), *Hotspur* (1986) and *Meeting the Comet* (1988), as well as her translations of medieval Latin lyrics, *The Virgin & the Nightingale* (1983). All her other collections were published by Oxford University Press until they shut down their poetry list in 1999, after which Bloodaxe published her collected poems, *Poems 1960-2000* (2000), followed by *Dragon Talk* (2010), *Glass Wings* (2013), *The Land Ballot* (2015) and *Hoard* (2017). *Poems 1960-2000* is a Poetry Book Society Special Commendation and *Glass Wings* a Poetry Book Society Recommendation.

the virgin and the nightingale

medieval latin poems
Fleur Adcock

BLOODAXE BOOKS

ISBN: 978 0 906427 56 9

First published 1983 by
Bloodaxe Books Ltd,
Eastburn,
South Park,
Hexham,
Northumberland NE46 1BS.

www.bloodaxebooks.com
For further information about Bloodaxe titles
please visit our website and join our mailing list
or write to the above address for a catalogue.

Supported using public funding by
**ARTS COUNCIL
ENGLAND**

Cover picture: Universitäts Bibliothek Heidelberg

Lettering and drawings: Peter Henry

This is a digital reprint of the 1983 Bloodaxe edition.

Acknowledgements

The author wishes to thank Peter Dronke for his encouragement and for permission to include the texts of three poems from his book *Medieval Latin and the Rise of European Love-Lyric*; acknowledgements are also due to Oxford University Press for the use of material from this work and from the *Oxford Book of Medieval Latin Verse*.

In addition the author is grateful to Northern Arts for financial support (as Fellow in Literature at the Universities of Newcastle upon Tyne and Durham) during the time when these translations were made, and to those universities for the congenial environment they provided.

Contents

birds

I.

Sunt saecla praeclarissima,
sunt prata vernantissima,
formosa gaudent omnia,
sunt grata nostri moenia.

Laetentur ergo somata
et rideant praecordia,
amor petens finitima
sint cuncta vitulantia.

Phoebus rotat per tempora
torquens polorum lumina;
somnum susurrant flumina,
aves canunt et dulcia.

Turtur prior dans oscina,
rauce sonat post ardea;
sistema miscens merula,
olos implet croëmata.

Myrto sedens lusciola,
'vos cara,' dicens, 'pignora,
audite matris famina,
dum lustrat aether sidera.

Cantans mei similia,
canora prolis germina,
cantu Deo dignissima
tractim refrange guttura.

Tu namque plebs laetissima,
tantum Dei tu psaltria
divina cantans cantica
per blanda cordis viscera.

Materna iam nunc formula
ut rostra vincas plumea,
futura vocis organa
contempera citissima.'

The singing-contest

We live in splendid times: the fields
are rich and blossoming with spring;
our city is a pleasant place;
there's joy in every living thing.

So let our bodies take their ease,
and hearts enjoy this happy state;
with 'love thy neighbour' as the theme
all creatures ought to celebrate.

The heavens wheel about the earth
with sun by day and stars at night;
the rivers whisper sleepily,
and singing birds express delight.

The cooing turtle-dove is first;
the heron follows with a squawk;
the blackbird joins the chorus; next
the swan contributes to their talk.

Then sitting on a myrtle branch
the nightingale instructs her young:
'Now while the stars are bright, my dears,
take lessons in your mother-tongue:

copy my song; I want to hear
the younger generation's notes
in seemly hymns of praise to God
emerging from your little throats.

We are a joyful tribe of birds,
the Lord's musicians and his choir.
So let him hear your instruments:
make every tiny chest a lyre.

Tune up your growing vocal chords
for instant use; adopt my skills
and we'll outdo what pass for songs
from other birds' inferior bills.'

Hoc dixit et mox iubila
secuntur subtilissima;
melum fit voce tinnula
soporans mentis intima.

Densantur hinc spectacula,
accurrit omnis bestia,
leaena, lynx et dammula,
caudata stans vulpecula.

Pisces relinquunt aequora
et vada sunt retrograda;
pulsando Codrus ilia
praegnas adest invidia.

Auro sedet rex aquila,
circum cohors per agmina,
gemmata pavo tergora,
cornix subest et garrula.

Corvina quin centuria,
ardet phalans et milvea;
de marte tractant omina,
vincatur ut lusciola.

Palumbes at iuvencula
praesumit e victoria;
gallus prior cum merula
disrumpta plangunt ilia.

Cicadis inflans iecora
campo crepat misellula;
palmam tenet lusciola
versus trahens per sibila.

Turbata gens tum rostrea,
exsanguis hinc et aquila;
frigescit, in praecordia
virtusque cedit ossea.

The youngsters do as they are told;
and soon their sweetly piping art
is mingled with their mother's tune
in melodies to stun the heart.

At this their audience expands,
as all the creatures flock to hear:
the little fox with bushy tail,
the lioness, lynx, and fallow deer.

Even the fishes leave the sea,
and rivers find their flow reversed;
the poet Codrus tears his hair,
so full of envy he could burst.

The eagle on a golden throne
presides above his marshalled rows
of peacocks dressed in jewelled gear,
and companies of chatty crows,

squadrons of kites, battalions
of ravens, all exchanging views
about the contest and its odds,
keen that the nightingale should lose.

But no: the ringdove has withdrawn,
despairing of the victory;
the cock and blackbird, ruptured both,
can only squeak with misery.

The cricket-bird inflates her lungs
and bursts with a pathetic pop.
The nightingale, with staying-power
to match her skill, comes out on top.

Dismay confounds the other birds;
the eagle's face is almost pale:
a ghastly chill invades his bones;
his very heartbeat seems to fail.

Praeco fugae fit ulula
urgens gradi per abdita,
pudore mens ne conscia
poenas luat per saecula.

Tunc versa castra plumea
sparsim legunt aumatia
auraeque fissa flamina,
petuntur tecta silvea.

The screech owl signals the retreat,
urging the birds to slip away,
or else the shame will haunt their minds
tormenting them till Judgement Day.

And so the feathered ranks disperse;
their whistling wings divide the air
as each escapes to find his own
secluded nook or leafy lair.

II.

Caput gemmato,   caeteris praeclarus;
mane consurgit,   admonet suos pares;
suave canet   ad monacharum aures.

Est nominatus   auriolus clarus;
in ulnis virdis,   pectus purpuratum
longum producit   sibilum per auras.

Plateo collo   et iacintina crura,
dorso crogato   et cauda galluca;
in quercu canet,   dum fratres manducant.

Giro se turnat,   in ramo iucundat;
respectu clarus,   lucet tamquam aurum;
ut laetus mimus,   tales facit risos.

Nido suspensus   ad suos pullones;
ut eum cernant   sui amatores,
cunctas praecellit   parvulorum voces.

Pedes turinos,   oculos praeclaros;
velox in pinnis,   voce modulatus;
sanctorum grege   dulciter amatus.

In vespertino   exultat garritu,
suave canet   monachis auditu,
solis occasu   redit ad secretum.

The golden oriole at the monastery

Most brilliant of birds   with his jewel-decked head
he rises early   and calls to the others;
sweetly he sings to   the ears of the brothers.

His noble name is   the golden oriole;
on the green branches,   his breast a bright dazzle,
he pierces the air   with a long-drawn whistle.

His neck is purple   and his legs hyacinth;
his back of saffron   with a bright yellow tail.
He sings in the oak   while the monks have their meal.

Turning somersaults   he clowns on the branches;
vivid from behind   he glitters like gold-leaf.
His happy antics   make all the monks laugh.

He hangs on the nest   above his young nestlings
showing himself off   to the admiring faces;
he can outsing all   his chicks' little voices.

His feet are golden   and his eyes are brilliant;
swift upon the wing,   expert in melody,
he has enchanted   the holy company.

He proclaims his joy   in the evening chorus
carolling sweetly   to the brothers' delight.
At sunset he hides   in his private retreat.

III.

Vox, philomela, tua cantus edicere cogit,
inde tui laudem rustica lingua canit.
Vox, philomela, tua citheras in carmine vincit
et superas miris musica flabra modis.

Vox, philomela, tua curarum semina pellit,
recreat et blandis anxia corda sonis.
Florea rura colis, herboso caespite gaudes,
frondibus arboreis pignera parva foves.

Cantibus ecce tuis recrepant arbusta canoris,
consonat ipsa suis frondea silva comis.
Iudice me cygnus et garrula cedat hirundo,
cedat et inlustri psittacus ore tibi.

Nulla tuos umquam cantus imitabitur ales,
murmure namque tuo dulcia mella fluunt.
Dic ergo tremulos lingua vibrante susurros
et suavi liquidum gutture pange melos.

Porrige dulcisonas attentis auribus escas;
nolo tacere velis, nolo tacere velis.
Gloria summa tibi, laus et benedictio, Christe,
qui praestas famulis haec bona grata tuis.

EUGENIUS OF TOLEDO *died 658*

The nightingale

Your voice, my nightingale, makes everyone a singer:
so people in the country sing your praise.
Your voice is an instrument finer than a zither;
more hauntingly than wind-music it plays.

Your voice, my nightingale, uproots the seeds of sorrow;
its silken tones can soothe a troubled mood.
Your home is among flowers, you love a grassy meadow;
in leafy trees you tend your infant brood.

Hear how your melodies re-echo in the thicket:
even the rustling branches harmonize.
The swan, the twittering swallow, the gaudy-headed parrot
can never hope to match you in my eyes.

No bird can imitate the sweetness of your singing;
there's honey in your fluent, rippling note.
Speak with your vibrant tongue, then, in soft shivery
    warbling,
pouring the liquid sounds from your smooth throat.

Feed our expectant ears with your song's delicious flavour;
never be silent, never silent, please!
Glory and blessing and praise to Christ our Saviour
who grants his servants pleasures such as these!

IV.

Clangam, filii,
ploratione una

alitis cygni,
qui transfretavit aequora.

O quam amare
lamentabatur, arida

se dereliquisse
florigera
et petisse alta
maria.

Aiens: infelix sum
avicula,
heu mihi, quid agam
misera?

Pennis soluta
inniti
lucida non potero
hic in stilla.

Undis quatior,
procellis
hinc inde nunc allidor
exsulata.

Angor inter arta
gurgitum cacumina
gemens alatizo
intuens mortifera,
non conscendens supera.

Cernens copiosa
piscium legumina,
non queo in denso
gurgitum assumere
alimenta optima.

The swan

Hear me, my children,
telling the lamentation

of the winged swan
who journeyed across the ocean.

Bitterly he grieved
for what he had abandoned —

the flowering meadows
of the solid land —
to make his voyage
over the high seas.

This was his cry:
'I am a doomed creature.
What shall I do
in my desperate misery?

My wings will never
support me freely
here in this brightly
clinging moisture.

The waves batter me,
the force of the gale
dashes me to and fro
in my exile.

I am confined between
close peaks of water.
Flying I moan
and gaze at the doom-bearers,
unable to mount higher.

I can see pasture
in plenty for fishes
but in the crowding billows
I cannot snatch a bite
for my own good nurture.

Ortus, occasus,
plagae poli,
administrate
lucida sidera.

Sufflagitate
Oriona,
effugitantes
nubes occiduas.

Dum haec cogitaret tacita,
venit rutila
adminicula aurora.

Oppitulata afflamine
coepit virium
recuperare fortia.

Ovatizans
iam agebatur
inter alta
et consueta nubium
sidera.

Hilarata
ac iucundata
nimis facta,
penetrabatur marium
flumina.

Dulcimode cantitans
volitavit ad amoena
arida.

Concurrite omnia
alitum et conclamate
agmina:

Regi magno
sit gloria.

Sunrise and sunset
and polar quarters,
give me for guidance
the brilliance of stars.

Summon Orion
to light my way.
Sweep the western
clouds from my vision.'

While these thoughts possessed his mind
vermilion dawn
came to his rescue.

A breeze gusted up for him,
making him strong
with his old vigour.

Now he exulted,
feeling himself flung
amid the stars
in their high familiar
constellations.

Joy overtook him;
he was ecstatic
beyond telling
as he dived and surfaced
in the streams of sea.

Singing his melodies
he glided to the welcome
shores of dry land.

Come now, all you multitudes
of birds, and proclaim
together in chorus:

Praise and glory
to the great King.

V.

Iam pridem nimium residebam maestus amoeno
pomerio chiram laevam positam subhabensque
ad malam nimia dentum pro morte doloris.
Vox subito turdi nostras tunc perculit aures
invalidas dulcis varios imitando volucres.
Ad sonitum galli resonabat gutture tenso;
post vero merulae morem milvique sonabat;
inde simul recinens velut aureolus nitidusque,
bitrisci vocem frangebat et ipse pusilli.
Talia demirans, confestim diffugit ultro
improbus ille dolor, qui me vexabat amare;
deinde petens nidum, memetque laborque revisit.
Quem Deus appellat, ne me torquere parumper
exim iam valeat, submisse flagito, noster.

FREDEGARD OF ST RIQUIER *c.825*

The thrush

I sat in a mild orchard, but had no pleasure there,
clutching my jaw to muffle pain I could hardly bear:
toothache made my senses wince; but suddenly I heard
the pretty thrush performing impressions, clever bird.
She stretched her throat and uttered a 'Cock-a-doodle-doo',
followed by the blackbird's tune and the kite's piercing
  mew.
Two notes in combination then issued from her bill:
the wren's miniature piping and the oriole's trill.
Stunned by this exhibition, my torment let me be:
its gnawing grip relented, and left my tooth pain-free.
Off to her nest the thrush went, and I took up my pen.
May God send her back to me if toothache strikes again!

VI.

Vestiunt silve tenera ramorum
virgulta, suis onerata pomis,
canunt de celsis sedibus palumbes
    carmina cunctis.

Hic turtur gemit, resonat hic turdus,
pangit hic priscus merulorum sonus;
passer nec tacet, arripens garritu
    alta sub ulmis.

Hic leta sedit philomela frondis;
longum effundit sibilum per auras
sollempne, milvus tremulaque voce
    aethera pulsat.

Ad astra volans aquila, per agros
alauda canit modulos quam plures;
desursum vergit dissimili modo,
    dum terram tangit.

Velox impulit iugiter hirundo,
clangit coturnix, gracula resultat;
aves sic cuncte celebrant estivum
    undique carmen.

Nulla inter aves similis est api,
que talem gerit tipum castitatis
nisi que Christum baiulavit alvo
    inviolata.

The birds and the bee

Now in the woodlands every slender branch is
dressed in its leaves, and bearing fruit or berries,
while from their perches high among the treetops
    pigeons are cooing.

Here is the crooning dove, the thrush's warbling;
here is the blackbirds' well-remembered chorus;
even the dunnock chirps its lowly twitter
    under the elmtrees.

Here in the leaves the nightingale is joyful,
pouring her long sweet whistle on the breezes;
meanwhile the kite's voice, quavering and vibrant,
    creaks through the heavens.

Up soars the eagle, aiming for the stars; while
lower the skylark floods the fields with music,
rising and swooping, plummeting to earthward
    in her own fashion.

Swiftly the swallow darts without alighting;
quails are heard calling, jackdaws make their clamour;
so all the birds are celebrating summer,
    all of them singing.

None of the birds is like the little bee, though —
model for maidens, chastity's example:
no, only she who once cocooned the Christ-child
    safe in her belly.

VII.

Iuvenilis lascivia
et amoris suspiria
tam sunt delectabilia
   qu' En Rosseinos en cante.

Hec est amoris nuncia,
et hec inflammat basia
et accendit incendia
   mei estus, que s'en vante.

Audivi sepe merulam
dum movet ignis stipulam
et hec pungit puellulam
   mil fiz desob quarante.

Que durior est marmure
et es habet in pectore
ut hanc audit sub arbore
   tut est rendeu ardante.

Hec est avis Cupidinis,
que post ictum harundinis
movet estus libidinis
   'oci! oci!' dum cante.

Love's agent

The courting of a girl and boy
who love and sigh and touch and toy
inflames the nightingale with joy:
   she has to trill and coo it.

She's love's announcer and town-crier;
she lights the spark and stokes the fire;
she swells the lover with desire,
   then boasts that he'll pursue it.

I've heard her in a leafy glade
encouraging some heated blade
to pierce a girl who was a maid —
   and countless times will rue it.

A lady may be made of stone,
her heart encased in bronze, not bone;
but when she hears this melting tone
   her body burns to do it.

The nightingale takes Cupid's part:
when he's installed the teasing dart
she makes the inflammation start
   by wanton warblings to it.

VIII.

Pulcher valet ver in silva,
                 florigera tempora,
quando humus fert erbarum
                 copia titanica,
vernat silva frondosarum
                 species virencia.

Ibi cantant tunc caterva
                 volucrum lustrancia,
ex quarum huna plus manet
                 corporis exigua,
nomen clara hac robusta
                 philomela nuncupat.

Salliendo nemorosa
                 petit alta silva dies
philomela titubando
                 arborum chacumina,
nocte numquam cessat densa
                 clangere armonia.

Prolixa non rauca mittit
                 voce sepe sibila,
plura canit incantando
                 saltuum prostibula,
gliscit mirabilis membra
                 ludens menia carmina.

O tu parva, cur non cessas
                 clangere, avicula?
Estimas nunc superare
                 omnes arte musica?
Aut quid cum lira contempnis
                 sonora dulciflua?

The anti-nightingale song

Pretty Spring has dressed the woodlands
          with her floral artistry,
while the earth brings forth its herbage
          in titanic quantity
and the leafy trees are loaded
          handsomely with greenery.

There a strolling company of
          vocalists is audible,
out of which one narrow-gutted
          little bird is notable,
making clear in sturdy accents
          that she's called the nightingale.

In the daytime she's retiring,
          fond of shady privacy:
off she tittups through the branches
          to the summit of a tree;
but at night she never ceases
          blaring out her melody.

Her incessant, not untuneful
          whistling voice is never mute,
as she chants her incantations
          like a woodland prostitute,
puffing up her puny figure
          full of music and conceit.

'Will you never stop that racket,
          overrated little bird?
Do you think your art surpasses
          all the singing ever heard?
Don't you know that other music
          is quite frequently preferred?

Ultra vires iocabunda
        luctas thimfanistria,
te auscultant vigilando
        regalis insignia,
laudat procerum caterva
        tua plura cantica.

Cessa, cessa fatigando
        lassata iam bucula,
quia premis dormizantes
        clam iugiter nausia,
omni ora pro quid canis
        digna ovans sidera?

Misera, infelix illa,
        tam tenuis viscera,
que nec tumes saciata
        opima cibaria,
speras cantizando cunctis
        imperare gracia?

Iam cessato laborando,
        non premitit brachia,
. . . te cuncti auscultant,
        nemo dat iuvamina
nisi ipse, qui te fincxit
        propria spiramina.

Parce vatem iam secura,
        heiulare tardita,
conticesce, conticesce,
        ne crepando clangita,
ancxiata vires nollis,
        locum tuum propera.

Illa vero stringens pauca
        modulorum garrita
in estate stupefacta
        pro natorum gloria.
Bruma tegit nebulosa
        corpus sua funera.

As you bash your tinkling cymbals
　　　　with excessive jollity
wakeful crowds of listening gentry
　　　　egg you on with flattery:
your eternal serenading
　　　　wins the praise of royalty.

Stop it, stop it, you're a nuisance—
　　　　surely now you've tired your beak?
When I try a little snoozing
　　　　on the sly, you make me sick.
Must you fill up every moment
　　　　with pretentious rhetoric?

Wretched, miserable birdlet,
　　　　with your skinny little chest,
you're not stuffed up like a gander
　　　　which has feasted on the best:
do you hope that through your warbling
　　　　all will bow to your behest?

Now a pause in the performance;
　　　　but you're singing on the cheap:
out of all who listen to you,
　　　　no one offers you a tip —
only God, perhaps, who made you
　　　　with his special workmanship.

Have some pity on a poet:
　　　　please control your nagging tongue;
shut your beak, and let's have silence
　　　　from that boring, jangling song.
Save your energies for later:
　　　　go off home where you belong!'

But in summer, what relief! She
　　　　gives her voice a little rest,
stupefied with admiration
　　　　of the offspring in her nest.
And when winter comes, she's vanished,
　　　　dead beneath the freezing mist.

33

Trinitas sancta superna
                    nostra purget crimina,
ut ad alta poli summi
                    introducat limina
regnareque nos concedat
                    per secla in aeterna. Amen.

Now may all our sins be pardoned
                by the blessed Trinity
so that we may enter Heaven
                in a state of sanctity
and be granted safe positions
                there throughout eternity.

IX.

Olim lacus colueram,
olim pulcher exstiteram,
dum cygnus ego fueram.
Miser! miser!
Modo niger
et ustus fortiter!

Eram nive candidior,
quavis ave formosior;
modo sum corvo nigrior.
Miser! miser!
Modo niger
et ustus fortiter!

Me rogus urit fortiter,
gyrat, regyrat garcifer;
propinat me nunc dapifer.
Miser! miser!
Modo niger
et ustus fortiter!

Mallem in aquis vivere,
nudo semper sub aere,
quam in hoc mergi pipere.
Miser! miser!
Modo niger
et ustus fortiter!

Nunc in scutella iaceo
et volitare nequeo;
dentes frendentes video —
Miser! miser!
Modo niger
et ustus fortiter!

The roasted swan

I used to live upon a lake,
as fine a bird as God could make:
I was a swan, and no mistake.
Alas, poor me!
Black as tinder
and burnt to a cinder!

In those days I was white as snow,
fairer than any bird I know;
but now I'm blacker than a crow.
Alas, poor me!
Black as tinder
and burnt to a cinder!

They spitted me before a fire;
the kitchen-boy revolved the gyre;
the butler bears me from my pyre.
Alas, poor me!
Black as tinder
and burnt to a cinder!

I'd rather live with no defence,
naked against the elements,
than drown in sauce and condiments.
Alas, poor me!
Black as tinder
and burnt to a cinder.

But now I'm stranded on a tray,
too overdone to fly away,
while chomping teeth await their prey.
Alas, poor me!
Black as tinder
and burnt to a cinder!

Songs by Peter of Blois

X.

Ex ungue primo teneram
    nutrieram
  ut te, Lice,
   prima vice
aetatem circa puberem
    exigerem
     et caperem
primitias pudoris!

Fovisti viros gremio
    propicio,
  iam iam vivis
  cum lascivis —
septennis adhuc fueras
    — te reseras —
    admiseras
illecebras amoris.

Me meo memini
scripsisse legem inguini —
  pro foribus astaret,
   nec molestum virgini
profundius intraret!

Audax virguncula
maiora multo iacula
  suscipere decrevit —
   votum, licet parvula,
femineum explevit.

   Pubertatem
   per etatem
   dum stultior
   operior,
    Lice! Lice!
Lice, sexu ducta femineo,
virgo virum nosti, et doleo,
doleo! doleo! doleo!

Lucy

I nursed you as a father would
        from babyhood,
    Lucy, till now,
    dreaming of how
soon, when you'd grown an inch or two
        I'd claim my due
        and plunge into
your freshly ripened treasure.

But I've been beaten to the claim;
        you're on the game,
    admitting men
    time and again —
seven years old when first you tried:
        you opened wide,
        it slipped inside,
that new toy for your pleasure.

    I'd made myself a rule,
I well remember, for my tool,
    nobly forcing it to wait
        outside in the vestibule,
    not to crash your virgin gate.

    But you, little delinq-
uent, you've invited men to sink
    huger, more delicious thrusts
        into that receptive chink,
    not too small for adult lusts.

        'Virginity
        till puberty':
        I was a fool
        to make that rule.
        Lucy, Lucy,
precocious child, you got the itch to try
games women play with men. It makes me cry,
    it makes me cry, truly makes me cry.

[Te futuram
iam maturam
dum studeo,
custidio,
    Lice! Lice!
corpus adhuc impube, tenerum,
furtim vendis, migrans, adulterum —
    doleo! doleo! doleo!]

With all my care
to be quite fair
and let you grow,
I was too slow;
    Lucy, Lucy,
my randy nymphet with the roving eye,
you sell your little body on the sly.
  It makes me cry, truly makes me cry.

XI.

Quam velim virginum,   si detur opcio,
consulti pectoris   utar iudicio.
Non vagam animo   non turpem faciam
thori participem   curarum sociam.
   Pudoris prodigam   non eligam
   nec Sabinam moribus   amoribus.

Non curo teneram   etate primula:
non arat sapiens   in tali vitula.
Est enim sacius   cognosse puberem,
que blandam senciat   ex equo Venerem.

Si ruga lineas   suas araverit,
senecta capiti   nives asperserit:
non declinaverim   ad eius gremium,
licet in purpura   redimat senium.
   Tam mea   tam meus
   deliciosus amor   deliciosa Venus.

His not impossible she

Which girl would I prefer   if I were free to choose?
My judgement and my heart   would both be asked their
                                                          views.
One with a shady past   and fancies in her head
won't qualify to share   my troubles and my bed.
     A girl who's overfree   is not for me:
     no Bohemian raver   gets my favour.

A tender little bud   with petals tightly shut
won't do: it isn't wise   to plough in such a rut.
Better if she's attained   her teens or even more:
an equal match in bed,   a girl who knows the score.

But if the years have lined   her face beyond repair,
and many winters thrown   a snowfall on her hair,
my rising sun will scorn   to set between her thighs,
no matter what fine gear   she wears as a disguise.
     Now you know,   now you see,
     how my delectable love,   my delicious dear, will be.

45

XII.

Grates ago Veneri,
    que prosperi
michi risus numine
    de virgine
       mea gratum
       et optatum
       contulit tropheum.

Dudum militaveram,
    nec poteram
hoc frui stipendio;
    nunc sentio
       me beari,
       serenari
       vultum Dioneum.

Visu, colloquio,
contactu, basio
frui virgo dederat;
    sed aberat
linea posterior
    et melior
       amori.
Quam nisi transiero,
    de cetero
sunt, que dantur alia,
    materia
       furori.

The conquest of Coronis

Thank you, Venus, from my heart!
    You took my part,
smiling on me graciously,
    and granted me
      this precious pearl,
      the lovely girl
    whom I've so long adored.

When I started my campaign
    I couldn't gain
victory; but on I fought
    and, blissful thought,
      my luck has turned:
      at last I've earned
    the goddess's reward.

To gaze, to talk, to touch,
to kiss: four things. So much
my sweet virgin would permit;
    but she'd omit
that one item on the list
    her optimist
      was craving:
which unless one can achieve
    the others leave
harrowing effects, and can
    send any man
      quite raving.

Ad metam propero.
Sed fletu tenero
mea me sollicitat,
    dum dubitat
solvere virguncula
    repagula
      pudoris.
Flentis bibo lacrimas
    dulcissimas;
sic me plus inebrio,
    plus haurio
      fervoris.

Delibuta lacrimis
oscula plus sapiunt,
blandimentis intimis
mentem plus alliciunt.
Ergo magis capior,
    et acrior
vis flamme recalescit.
Sed dolor Coronidis
    se tumidis
exerit singultibus
    nec precibus
      mitescit.

Preces addo precibus
basiaque basiis;
fletus illa fletibus,
iurgia conviciis,
meque cernit oculo
    nunc emulo,
nunc quasi supplicanti;
nam nunc lite dimicat,
    nunc supplicat;
dumque prece blandior,
    fit surdior
      precanti.

I press towards my goal;
but she, the timid soul,
disconcerts me with her tears:
        Coronis fears
to unlock her virgin shrine
        for loving's fine
                completeness.
Lovely tears! I drink them all
        before they fall;
they intoxicate my brain
        the more I drain
                their sweetness.

Kisses wet with salty dew
have a more exciting taste;
they inflame me through and through,
firing me with urgent haste.
Thus her weeping stokes the fires
        as my desire's
fed by her teardrops' flavour.
But my darling's too distressed —
        her heaving breast
racked with sobs — to yield to me
        and hear my plea
                with favour.

I redouble my appeals,
backed with kisses by the score;
she weeps twice as hard, and deals
more reproaches than before.
She regards me with an eye
        now coldly dry,
now moist with anxious pleading.
First she battles for release,
        then begs for peace.
But when I cajole and pray
        she turns away
                unheeding.

Vim nimis audax infero.
Hec ungue sevit aspero,
 comas vellit,
 vim repellit
  strenua,
 sese plicat
 et intricat
  genua,
 ne ianua
pudoris resolvatur.

Sed tandem ultra milito,
triumphum do proposito.
 Per amplexus
 firmo nexus,
  brachia
 eius ligo,
 pressa figo
  basia;
 sic regia
Diones reseratur.

Res utrique placuit,
et me minus arguit
mitior amasia,
  dans basia
   mellita.

Et subridens tremulis
semiclausis oculis,
veluti sub anxio
  suspirio
   sopita.

I boldly bring some force to bear;
it doesn't work: she grabs my hair
        and beats me back;
        her nails attack
            viciously.
        She grimly blocks
        my access, locks
            knee with knee,
        and will not free
the gateway to her treasure.

But nonetheless I soldier on;
at last her opposition's gone!
        With tighter hold
        my arms enfold
            hers; I pin
        her down, and kiss
        my captive. This
            lets me in;
        and so I win
admission to love's pleasure.

Both of us enjoy the act;
and my love, with gentle tact,
doesn't chide, but kisses me
        deliciously,
            sweet and deep.

Then she offers me a smile,
somewhat tremblingly; and while
leaning back with half-closed eyes
        she faintly sighs,
            falls asleep.

XIII.

O cunctis liberalior,
cuius amore morior,
  ne moriar amore,
fias amanti micior!
Des ut agam, qui pacior,
  sine protractu more!

Dum, quod expectem, moneor,
et blanda voce moveor
  et dulcibus responsis.
Et expectarem, fateor;
sed expectare vereor,
  donec solvendo non sis.

Non horam certam nominas,
sed moras perdiutinas
  me protrahis invito.
'Erit, erit' ingeminas
et termino determinas
  tempus indefinito.

Cum cauis surget angulis
presectis rigens stipulis
  iam barba, non lanugo,
pilorum pungar iaculis
et tunc offendar osculis,
  que nunc libenter sugo.

Quod adhuc places pauculis,
solis debes novaculis.
  Sis ergo memor evi!
Non parcit evum singulis
nec breve regnum populis:
  nec parce regno brevi!

A friendly warning

You're nice to everyone but me.
I'm dying for you, can't you see?
    Don't let me die of yearning!
Be kinder to your devotee:
allow me some activity
    instead of passive burning!

Just waiting's what you advocate,
in winning tones which captivate
    and sweetly charm the ear;
and I admit I ought to wait;
but waiting's an unhappy state
    unless the outcome's clear.

You never firmly name the day,
but everlastingly delay
    and rack me with frustration.
'The time will come' you often say.
The time does not: it slips away
    in vague procrastination.

But shortly bristles will declare
that what your shapely features wear
    is beard, and not just fluff;
and stabbed by needle-tips of hair
I'll shudder then to kiss you where
    I now can't kiss enough.

If up to now you've quite a few
admirers, that's entirely due
    to youth; but hear my warning!
Old age will come; the years accrue
to one and all, and won't spare you.
    Enjoy life's precious morning!

Quid regno forme brevius
et forma quid infirmius
    est in sexu virili?
Nempe cogunt, ut cicius
matre senescat filius,
    non tempora sed pili.

Sic me solari solitus
cum de te bonos exitus
    sponderes in futuro,
tunc eram tibi deditus.
Nunc es miles emeritus;
    nunc de te minus curo.

Iam mea querit servitus
in libertatem reditus.
    Iam, iam me manumittas!
Prius te perdam penitus,
quam Licino te primitus
    et michi post submittas.

Parce, precor, et, quoniam
pecco per inpericiam,
    peccatum non require.
Quos urget ad iniuriam,
pro his Amor ad veniam
    debet intervenire.

Me procul a me statuit
Amor et interposuit
    se mee rationi.
Ergo lingua quid potuit,
cognata si non habuit
    verba discrecioni?

The reign of beauty's quickly done;
and if the so far beauteous one
	is male, then he's in trouble:
old age descends upon a son
before his mother's has begun.
	The cause? Not years, but stubble.

You used to soothe me, telling how
before much longer you'd allow
	the joys I was awaiting.
Then I was yours; I'd made a vow.
But you're an old campaigner now;
	and now my love's abating.

Already now my slavery
would like to change to liberty.
	Make haste, and set me free!
I'd rather lose you totally
than have you yield initially
	to shaving, then to me.

Forgive me if in any sense
I sin through inexperience:
	don't be too much aggrieved.
Since love makes lovers give offence,
love ought to come to their defence
	and see that they're reprieved.

It's love that has removed my heart
some distance from my thinking part:
	hence my insane caprices.
But love, like language, couldn't start
to work for us without the art
	of coupling separate pieces.

XIV.

Predantur oculos, captivant animum
       vocalis Orphei
         siderei
vultus et simplices   risus Euridices.

   Qui solis animos   luneque menstruos
      rimari solitus
       circuitus,
    celo fugam siderum
      per numerum
       notatam,

iam nunc ad alteram   traductus operam,
    mutato studio,
     de basio,
    de amplexu loquitur
     et sequitur
      amatam.

In flammam abiit totus philosophus,
     amantis spiritum
      solicitum
tacente cithara   stupebant Ismara.

    Non vult Euridice
     de suplice;
preces perdat vacuas —
    sed ianuas
     pudoris
    et gremium
    dat pervium
    discursibus
    et lusibus
     amoris.

Orpheus

The singer Orpheus is totally beguiled:
    Eurydice's bright face
    and laughing grace
have won his eyes and heart   and lured him from his art.

He used to scrutinize   the movements of the skies:
    the cyclic moon, the sun
    fixed in its run,
    planets, and the zodiac's
    established tracks
    and motion.

But now his urge to learn   has taken a new turn:
    he studies kissing now,
    and talks of how
    he'll embrace his new pursuit
    with absolute
    devotion.

The once philosopher has quite gone up in flames.
    The people stand amazed
    to see him dazed
by passion, with his lyre   untouched in his desire.

    For weeks Eurydice
    ignores his plea:
    she's averse to being wooed;
    but then her mood
    grows tender,
    and on a whim
    she offers him
    her secret gift
    in ardent, swift
    surrender.

Sumpto libamine
de virgine,
suam tandem fidicen
Euridicen
cognovit,
et lirico
sub cantico
iam spiritum
sollicitum
removit.

He takes her virgin flower;
        she's in his power
wholly of her own sweet will.
    He drinks his fill
        with gladness,
    and tunes his lyre
    with sudden fire
    to play a strain
    that ends the reign
        of sadness.

XV

Sevit aure spiritus
   et arborem
come fluunt penitus
   vi frigorum;
silent cantus nemorum.
Nunc torpescit vere solo
   fervens amor pecorum:
semper amans sequi nolo
   novas vices temporum
     bestiali more.
     En gaudia   felicia!
     Quam dulcia   stipendia
     sunt hec hore   nostre Flore!

Non de longo conqueror
   obsequio;
nobili remuneror
   stipendio;
leto letor premio.
Dum salutat me loquaci
   Flora supercilio:
mente satis non capaci
   gaudia concipio,
     glorior labore.
     En gaudia, etc.

Michi sors obsequitur
   non aspera.
Dum secreta luditur
   in camera,
favet Venus prospera.
Nudam fovet Floram lectus;
   caro candet tenera;
virginale lucet pectus
   parum surgunt ubera
     modico tumore.
     En gaudia, etc.

Flora

Now the winter's rages freeze
    the air, and drum
all the foliage from the trees
    when storm-winds hum.
In the woods the birds are dumb:
only spring excites their urges;
    winter turns all creatures numb.
My love's changeless, though: it surges
    through whatever seasons come,
        constantly renewing.
        See what rewards   my love affords!
        I couldn't ask   a sweeter task
        than pursuing   what I'm doing.

Mine's no weary courtship, slow
    and full of sighs,
bleakly unrewarding. No:
    my enterprise
earns a rich and noble prize.
When my Flora signals to me
    with her fine expressive eyes
joy and triumph eddy through me;
    just what rapture they imply's
        far beyond my knowing.
        See what rewards, etc.

Fate indulges me: my case
    is sanctified.
Playing in our secret place
    we've cause for pride:
Venus is our willing guide.
Flora lies, all shining whiteness,
    pure and naked by my side,
dazzling in her virgin brightness
    with her body still untried,
        tender breasts just growing.
        See what rewards, etc.

A tenello tenera
     pectusculo
distenduntur latera
     pro modulo;
caro carens scrupulo
lenem tactum non offendit.
  Gracilis sub cingulo
umbilicum preextendit
  paululum ventriculo
    tumescentiore.
     En gaudia, etc.

Vota blando stimulat
     lenimine
pubes, que vix pullulat
     in virgine
tenui lanugine.
Crus vestitum moderata
  tenerum pinguedine
levigatur occultata
  nervorum compagine
    radians candore.
     En gaudia, etc.

Hominem transgredior
     et superum
sublimari glorior
     ad numerum:
sinum tractans tenerum
cursu vago dum beata
  manus it et uberum
regionem pervagata
  descendit ad uterum
    tactu leniore.
     En gaudia, etc.

Then, below that region graced
            with pretty twin
domes, she tapers to her waist,
            well-shaped and thin.
Not a blemish mars her skin,
not a hint of imperfection.
Further down her curves begin
rising to the slight projection
    of her little belly, in
        roundness barely showing.
            See what rewards, etc.

Hopes of promised pleasure fill
            my veins with heat;
here's her fluffy mound (she's still
            so young, her sweet
thatch of down's not quite complete).
Just correctly plump, her slender
    legs and thighs are smooth and neat,
slightly fuller at the tender
        secret junction where they meet,
            radiantly glowing.
            See what rewards, etc.

What I feel is too sublime
            to be expressed;
no one but a god could climb
            to such a crest.
Now my hand's divinely blessed:
first it wanders lightly glancing
    here and there about her breast,
then proceeds below, advancing
        down her belly to what's best,
            lovingly pursuing.
            See what rewards, etc.

O si forte Jupiter
      hanc videat,
timeo, ne pariter
      incaleat
et ad fraudes redeat:
sive Danen pluens aurum
      imbre dulci mulceat
vel Europes intret taurum
      vel Ledeo candeat
      rursus in olore.
En gaudia   *felicia!*
Quam dulcia   *stipendia*
sunt hec hore   *nostre Flore!*

I'm afraid if Jupiter
        should chance to spy
this, he'd be on fire for her
        as much as I:
he'd revert to all his sly
tricks; he'd try to rape her in a
    golden shower from the sky,
turn into a bull to win her,
    or (it worked with Leda) try
    swan-form for his wooing.
        See what rewards   my love affords!
        I couldn't ask   a sweeter task
        than pursuing   what I'm doing.

XVI.

Plaudit humus Boree
fugam ridens exulis.
Pullulant arboree
nodis come patulis.
Gaudet Rea coronari
   novis frontem flosculis,
olim gemens carcerari
   nivis sevis vinculis.
Felix morbus, qui sanari
nescit sine morbo pari.

Ethera Favonius
induit a vinculis.
Ornat mundum Cyprius
sacris dive copulis.
Castra Venus renovari
   novis ovat populis
et tenellas copulari
   blandis mentes stimulis.
Felix morbus, qui sanari
nescit sine morbo pari.

Tuum, Venus, haurio
venis ignem bibulis.
Tuis, Flora, sicio
favum de labellulis.
Flora, flore singulari
   preminens puellulis,
solum sola me solari
   soles in periculis.
Felix morbus, qui sanari
nescit sine morbo pari.

Peter's lament

People celebrate, at ease
now that winter's driven out;
on the newly verdant trees
frilly knobs of blossom sprout.
Earth's bedecked with cheerful frondage,
waving wreaths of buds about,
after lying long in bondage
chained by winter's icy drought.
Love's a wound that for its healing
needs a fellow-sufferer's feeling.

Enter now the western breeze,
putting mist and clouds to flight;
enter Venus, who decrees
all her creatures should unite,
male with female, in communion,
following their appetite;
people, too, are linked in union,
urged by her to love's delight.
Love's a wound that for its healing
needs a fellow-sufferer's feeling.

Through my veins I feel the hot
runnels of divine desire;
Flora's mouth's the honey-pot
which alone can quench my fire.
Flora, flower of uniqueness,
perfect pattern all admire,
only you can salve my weakness
with the succour I require.
Love's a wound that for its healing
needs a fellow-sufferer's feeling.

Rapit nobis ludere
dictis livor emulis,
nos obliquis ledere
gaudens lingue iaculis.
Nolo volens absentari,
votis uror pendulis.
Fugi, timens te notari
nigris fame titulis.
Felix morbus, qui sanari
nescit sine morbo pari.

In discessu dulcibus
non fruebar osculis.
Salutabas nutibus
pene loquens garrulis.
Fas non erat pauca fari.
Fuere pro verbulis,
quas, heu, vidi dirivari
lacrimas ex oculis.
Felix morbus, qui sanari
nescit sine morbo pari.

Envy with its bilious tongue
drove us from our tender play;
hypocrites and gossips flung
cutting weapons at their prey.
Now we burn in separation;
all my being longed to stay,
but to save your reputation
I was forced to go away.
Love's a wound that for its healing
needs a fellow-sufferer's feeling.

Rather anything than part
with no kiss; but it was so:
what was in your silent heart
only gestures dared to show.
Words were banned; but your revealing
eyes and features let me know
all the pain you were concealing
when your tears began to flow.
Love's a wound that for its healing
needs a fellow-sufferer's feeling.

XVII.

Dum iuventus floruit,
licuit   et libuit
facere, quod placuit,
    iuxta voluntatem
currere,   peragere
carnis voluptatem.

Amodo sic agere,
vivere   tam libere,
talem vitam ducere
    viri vetat etas,
perimit   et eximit
    leges assuetas.

Etas illa monuit,
docuit,   consuluit,
sic et etas annuit:
    'Nichil est exclusum!'
Omnia   cum venia
    contulit ad usum.

Volo resipiscere,
linquere,   corrigere,
quod commisi temere;
    deinceps intendam
seriis,   pro vitiis
    virtutes rependam.

A new leaf

While my youth was fresh and green
my routine   was quite serene:
all was pleasure; I was keen
    on the scent of action,
quick to chase   and then embrace
    carnal satisfaction.

Now my age begins to tell:
raising hell   's all very well,
but the middle years compel
    sober introspection;
then a man   will try to plan
    changes of direction.

Youth advised me to be free —
actively   encouraged me;
when I ventured on a spree
    there was no restriction:
'Go ahead,'   my conscience said,
    with its benediction.

Now it's time for penitence,
continence   and abstinence;
now I want to learn some sense;
    henceforth I'll be graver:
I'll go straight,   and cultivate
    ways to Heaven's favour.

anonymous love-songs

XVIII.

De ramis cadunt folia,
nam viror totus periit;
iam calor liquit omnia
    et habiit,
nam signa celi ultima
    sol peciit.

Iam nocet frigus teneris
et avis bruma leditur,
et Filomena ceteris
    conqueritur
quod illis ignis eteris
    adimitur.

·Nec limpha caret alveus
nec prata virent erbida;
sol nostra fugit aureus
    confinia:
est inde dies niveus,
    nox frigida.

Modo frigescit quiquid est,
sed solus ego caleo,
immo sic michi cordi est
    quod ardeo —
hic ignis tamen virgo est
    qua langeo.

Nutritur ignis osculo
et leni tactu virginis:
in suo lucet occulo
    lux luminis
nec est in toto seculo
    plus numinis.

The lover in winter

The leaves are falling; summer's past;
what once was green is brown and sere;
all nature's warmth has faded fast
　　and gone from here;
the circling sun has reached the last
　　house in its year.

Now fragile creatures feel the sting
of winter, and the birds complain:
led by the nightingale, they sing
　　in cold and pain
that heaven's fire is vanishing
　　from their domain.

The riverbeds resound with spray;
the grassy meadows now are white;
the golden sun has fled away
　　beyond our sight,
and left our land with snow by day
　　and frost by night.

The world is chilled in every part;
but I alone am warm, and grow
still warmer. It delights my heart
　　to feel this glow:
my lady made the burning start —
　　I love her so.

This holy fire is nourished by
her kisses and her gentle touch;
and shining from her radiant eye
　　the light is such
that neither earth nor brilliant sky
　　can show as much.

Ignis grecus extinguitur
cum vino iam acerrimo,
sed iste non extinguitur
    miserrimo,
immo fomento alitur
    uberrimo.

Greek fire can be put out, it's true,
by vinegar or sour wine;
but bitter quenchings can't subdue
   this fire of mine:
they nourish it to spring anew
   more bright and fine.

XIX.

Levis exsurgit zephirus,
et sol procedit tepidus,
iam terra sinus aperit,
dulcore suo diffluit.

Ver purpuratum exiit,
ornatus suos induit,
aspergit terram floribus,
ligna silvarum frondibus.

Struunt lustra quadrupedes
et dulces nidos volucres,
inter ligna florentia
sua decantant gaudia.

Quod oculis dum video
et auribus dum audio,
heu pro tantis gaudiis
tantis inflor suspiriis.

Cum mihi sola sedeo
et hec revolvens palleo,
si forte capud sublevo,
nec audio nec video.

Tu saltim, veris gratia,
exaudi et considera
frondes, flores et gramina,
nam mea languet anima.

The love-sick girl in spring

The breeze is gentle from the west,
the sun begins to warm the air;
and now the earth's uncovered breast
exudes its sweetness everywhere.

Spring has arrived, ornately gowned,
as if in jewels and brocade;
she scatters flowers on the ground
and clothes the trees with leafy shade.

The furry creatures dig their lairs;
the birds make nests, and sweetly sing
on blossom-studded boughs, in pairs,
of how they glory in the spring.

But though I hear them with my ears
and see them with my outward eyes,
none of these pretty doings cheers
my spirit; I am filled with sighs.

I sit alone, with senses dead
and thoughts awhirl; my face is pale;
and if I chance to lift my head
my sight and hearing seem to fail.

But you at least, my love, should yield
to Spring's attractions: be aware
of leaf and bud and flowered field;
my own soul is too sick to care.

XX.

Nil proponens temere
diligebam tenere,
quam sciebam degere
   sub etate tenera,
nil audens exigere
   preter mentis federa.

Iam etas invaluit,
iam amor incaluit;
iam virgo maturuit,
   iam tumescunt ubera;
iam frustra complacuit,
   nisi fiant cetera.

Ergo iunctis mentibus
iungamur corporibus!
Mellitis amplexibus
   fruamur cum gaudio!
Flos pre cunctis floribus,
   colluctemur serio!

Uvam dulcem premere,
mel de favo sugere:
quid hoc sit, exponere
   tibi, virgo, cupio;
non verbo, sed opere
   fiat expositio!

A touch of impatience

I was patient at the start,
full of diplomatic art;
you were young: I played my part
   with delicate good taste;
asking nothing but your heart
   I kept our courtship chaste.

Now you've reached a riper stage;
now the fire begins to rage;
now my virgin's come of age,
   with breasts new-grown and waiting —
wasted if we don't engage
   in something less frustrating.

Since we've coupled mind with mind
let's be physically entwined:
wrestling's a delight, you'll find,
   if you'll relax your guard.
Sweetest flower of all, be kind:
   let's play with no holds barred!

Grapes are luscious things to squeeze;
sucking honey's nice for bees.
What's my meaning? Darling, please
   accept a full translation:
not in language; what you'll see's
   a graphic demonstration.

XXI.

Amor habet superos:
  Iovem amat Iuno;
motus premens efferos
  imperat Neptuno;
Pluto tenens inferos
  mitis est hoc uno.
    Amoris solamine
    virgino cum virgine;
    aro non in semine,
    pecco sine crimine.

Amor trahit teneros
  molliori nexu,
rigidos et asperos
  duro frangit flexu;
capitur rhinoceros
  virginis amplexu.
    Amoris solamine, etc.

Virgo cum virginibus
  horreo corruptas,
et cum meretricibus
  simul odi nuptas;
nam in istis talibus
  turpis est voluptas.
    Amoris solamine, etc.

Virginis egregie
  ignibus calesco
et eius cotidie
  in amore cresco;
sol est in meridie,
  nec ego tepesco.
    Amoris solamine, etc.

Cecily

Love controls the gods themselves:
   Hera loves her Zeus;
love can calm Poseidon's rage,
   ordering a truce;
even Hell's grim ruler turns
   mild with love's excuse.
      I'm in love, but she's taboo,
      so with her I'm virgin too:
      legal action won't ensue
      if just flirting's all we do.

Love imprisons gentle souls
   in a tender trap;
tougher victims are restrained
   by a tighter strap.
Unicorns capitulate
   in a virgin's lap.
      I'm in love, etc.

Defloration is a sin —
   such a horrid thought!
Prostitution's just as bad:
   sex should not be bought.
As a virgin I detest
   sordid kinds of sport.
      I'm in love, etc.

My beloved's chaste and pure;
   day by day I grow
more in love; her virgin charms
   make my senses glow.
In the sky the sun's ablaze;
   I am warm below.
      I'm in love, etc.

Gratus super omnia
　　ludus est puelle,
et eius precordia
　　omni carent felle;
sunt, que prestat, basia
　　dulciora melle.
　　　　　Amoris solamine, etc.

Ludo cum Cecilia;
　　nichil timeatis!
Sum quasi custodia
　　fragilis etatis,
ne marcescant lilia
　　sue castitatis.
　　　　　Amoris solamine, etc.

Flos est; florem frangere
　　non est res secura,
uvam sino crescere,
　　donec sit matura;
spes me facit vivere
　　letum re ventura.
　　　　　Amoris solamine, etc.

Volo tantum ludere,
　　id est: contemplari,
presens loqui, tangere,
　　tandem osculari;
quintum, quod est agere,
　　noli suspicari!
　　　　　Amoris solamine, etc.

Quicquid agant ceteri,
　　virgo, sic agamus,
ut, quem decet fieri,
　　ludum faciamus;
ambo sumus teneri;
　　tenere ludamus!
　　　　　Amoris solamine, etc.

Playing with a little girl:
  that's the nicest game;
in her heart you'll never find
  bitterness or blame;
honey's not as sweet as these
  kisses that I claim.
    I'm in love, etc.

When I play with Cecily
  don't have any fears:
I'm a careful guardian
  of her tender years;
on her lily chastity
  not a mark appears.
    I'm in love, etc.

Picking flowers such as her
  makes one insecure;
so I leave the growing vine
  till the grape's mature.
Hopes of blissful times to come
  help me to endure.
    I'm in love, etc.

All I want to do is play.
  What I mean is this:
first to gaze, and then to talk,
  next to touch and kiss.
Any thoughts of item five
  totally dismiss!
    I'm in love, etc.

Let's do what the others do,
  but in such a way,
Cecily, that our delights
  don't lead us astray.
While we're children, childishly
  is the way to play.
    I'm in love, etc.

XXII.

Cum Fortuna voluit
      me vivere beatum,
forma, bonis moribus,
      fecit bene gratum
et in altis sedibus
      sedere laureatum.

Modo flos preteriit
      mee iuventutis,
in se trahit omnia
      tempus senectutis;
inde sum in gratia
      novissime salutis.

Rhinoceros virginibus
      se solet exhibere;
sed cuius est virginitas
      intemerata vere,
suo potest gremio
      hunc sola retinere.

Igitur que iuveni
      virgo sociatur
et me senem spreverit
      iure defraudatur,
ut ab hac rhinoceros
      se capi patiatur.

In tritura virginum
      debetur seniori
pro mercede palea,
      frumentum iuniori;
inde senex aream
      relinquo successori.

Farewell to the threshing-floor

Fortune used to smile on me:
         I didn't have to try;
good looks and charming manners
         were mine in full supply;
she crowned my head with laurels,
         and set me up on high.

But now my youth has faded;
         I've seen its petals fall;
time has brought old age to me,
         the latest phase of all;
now my final state of health
         has me in its thrall.

The unicorn's a shy beast,
         which virgins can allure;
but only she whose chastity's
         unchallengeably pure
can hold the creature in her lap
         and keep him there secure.

Therefore when a virgin girl
         has dealings with a boy,
spurning my mature advances,
         let her have her joy:
she'll never be successful as
         a unicorn's decoy.

At threshing-time for virgins,
         when harvesting's complete,
all an old man gets is chaff:
         the young man gets the wheat.
Let my successor wield the flail:
         I admit defeat.

Sources

The Latin texts of the poems are taken from:

Die Arundel Sammlung mittellateinischer Lieder [Arundel Collection], edited by Wilhelm Meyer (Berlin, 1908).

Die Cambridger Lieder [Cambridge Songs], edited by Karl Strecker (Berlin, 1955).

Carmina Burana, edited by A. Hilka and O. Schumann (Heidelberg, 1930–1941).

Peter Dronke, *Medieval Latin and the Rise of European Love-Lyric*, second edition (Oxford, 1968).

The Oxford Book of Medieval Latin Verse, edited by Stephen Gaselee (Oxford, 1928).

The Oxford Book of Medieval Latin Verse, edited by F. J. E. Raby (Oxford, 1959).

Wherever possible I have given references to Raby's Oxford Book (1959), as this is the most readily available anthology and includes further notes on some of the poems.

In addition to Helen Waddell's books (*The Wandering Scholars* and *Mediaeval Latin Lyrics*), other important works on the subject are:

Peter Dronke, *The Medieval Lyric*, second edition (London, 1978).

F. J. E. Raby, *A History of Secular Latin Poetry in the Middle Ages* (Oxford, 1934).

A note on the spelling of my Latin texts, in which some inconsistency will be detected: in his anthology Dr Raby chose to present most of the poems in 'the familiar spelling of classical Latin', and in those cases where I have taken my texts from that volume I have let his spelling stand. The other poems, however, are in the original spelling of the medieval manuscripts; this differs from classical Latin in a number of details, the most obvious of which is that the diphthong 'ae' has disappeared and been replaced by 'e'. Medieval Latin also varies from author to author and according to the traditions of different periods.

Notes on the poems

I.   *Oxford Book* (1959) no.100. *Circa* 900 A.D.; sometimes attributed to Eugenius Vulgarius but probably not his. Following Gaselee in his 1928 *Oxford Book* I have omitted the first stanza of the poem, which is merely a technical note on the verse-form.

II.   *Oxford Book* (1959) no.106. Anonymous, 10th century.

III.   *Oxford Book* (1959) no.62. The nightingale held a special place in medieval affections and in the lore of the time. A number of poems were written in its praise, and it was particularly associated with love (see poem VII).

IV.   *Oxford Book* (1959) no.68. Anonymous, 9th century. This poem, in sequence form, is an allegory of the soul's journey.

V.   *Oxford Book* (1959) no.82. I have translated only the first 14 lines of the poem.

VI.   *Cambridge Songs* no.23. I have used the text given by Raby in his *Oxford Book* (1959) no.124.

VII.   Dronke, *Medieval Latin and the Rise of European Love-Lyric*, II, p.361. Anonymous, 12th century.

VIII.   This piece of doggerel appears as no.1 in the appendix to Strecker's edition of the *Cambridge Songs*. It is a parody of no.10 in the collection, which praises the nightingale's musical talents in great detail; both poems are in the same form, in sixteen stanzas, and there are frequent verbal echoes in the parody. The text is somewhat conjectural here and there, which allows a modest amount of freedom to the translator at these points. I have omitted the first four stanzas, in praise of God the creator, but have included the final one, with its pleasing note of hypocrisy.

IX.   *Carmina Burana* no.130. 12th century.

X.   Dronke, *Medieval Latin and the Rise of European Love-Lyric*, II, p.378.

Peter of Blois (*c.* 1135-*c.* 1212) was a scholar and diplomat who acted as political secretary to Henry II and later to his widow Eleanor of Aquitaine; for an account of his work see

'Peter of Blois and poetry at the court of Henry II', by Peter Dronke in *Medieval Studies* 38 (1976), which convincingly attributes to this author a number of poems previously regarded as anonymous (including this one.)

As these lyrics were intended for singing I have adhered to the original metres and rhyme-schemes as closely as possible in my versions.

XI.   *Arundel Collection* no.28.

XII.   *Arundel Collection* no.10; *Carmina Burana* no.72. I can scarcely approve of the content of this poem, which describes something suspiciously close to rape, but I was unable to resist the challenge of its intricate form.

XIII.   *Arundel Collection* no.13. This is something of a departure for Peter of Blois, whose clear personal preference was for young females; Dronke sees it as a parody or burlesque.

XIV.   Dronke, *Medieval Latin and the Rise of European Love-Lyric*, II, p.403.

XV.   *Arundel Collection* no.8.

XVI.   *Arundel Collection* no.7. The initial letters of the stanzas form an acrostic of the author's name.

XVII.   *Carmina Burana* no.30.

XVIII.   *Oxford Book* (1959) no.234. Anonymous, before 1200. I have used the more authentic text given by Dronke, *Medieval Latin and the Rise of European Love-Lyric*, I, p.288.

XIX.   *Cambridge Songs* no.40; *Oxford Book* (1959) no.123. 11th century or earlier.

XX.   *Carmina Burana* no.167 II. 12th century.

XXI.   *Carmina Burana* no.88. 12th century.

XXII.   *Carmina Burana* no.93a. 12th century.

Printed in the USA
CPSIA information can be obtained
at www.ICGtesting.com
JSHW082223140824
68134JS00015B/707